Sports Illustrated KIDS

T0103160

THE STORY OF SOCCER

BY NICK HUNTER

CAPSTONE PRESS
a capstone imprint

Published by Capstone Press, an imprint of Capstone
1710 Roe Crest Drive, North Mankato, Minnesota 56003
capstonepub.com

SPORTS ILLUSTRATED KIDS is a trademark of ABG-SI LLC. Used with permission.

Library of Congress Cataloging-in-Publication Data is available on the Library of Congress website.
ISBN: 9781669076087 (hardcover)
ISBN: 9781669076032 (paperback)
ISBN: 9781669076049 (ebook pdf)

Summary: How did soccer become the world's most popular sport with billions of fans and millions
of players? From its earliest beginnings to the most recent World Cup winners, readers will find out
unforgettable facts about their favorite sport!

Editor: Erika L. Shores; Designer: Sofiia Rovinskaia; Media Researcher: Jo Miller; Production Specialist:
Tori Abraham

Image Credits
Alamy: Daniel Motz, 21, dpa picture alliance, 15, 27, Mirrorpix/Trinity Mirror, 19, PA Images, 13, 17,
ZUMA Press, Inc., 28; Associated Press: picture-alliance/dpa, 11; Getty Images: AfricaImages, 29, Hulton
Archive, 9, Mike Powell, 20, Naomi Baker, 5, Simon Bruty, 23; Shutterstock: FocusStocker, Cover (top);
Sports Illustrated: Erick W. Rasco, 26, Peter Read Miller, Cover (bottom right), Simon Bruty, Cover
(bottom left), 25; Superstock: Universal Images/Pictures from History, 7

Design Elements:
Shutterstock: Gojindbefs, Kucher Serhii (football), Lifestyle Graphic, Navin Penrat

Printed and bound in China. 5827

TABLE OF CONTENTS

Words in BOLD are in the glossary.

THE GLOBAL GAME

Visit almost any country in the world and you will find people playing soccer. You might see a group of kids kicking a ball around on a scrubby patch of land. Or it might be a **professional** game watched by thousands of fans in a stadium and millions more watching it on TV.

One reason for soccer's popularity is that it can be played almost anywhere. All you need is an area of mostly flat ground, a ball, and something to mark goals. Players don't need to be particularly tall or strong. If you can kick the ball, you can play and learn the skills you need. Soccer games for people with disabilities mean that everyone can play.

More than 250 million people play organized soccer around the world. Where did the game come from and how did it become the world's most popular sport?

In 2022, Germany and England faced each other in the Women's Euros final.

THE ORIGINS OF SOCCER

The first game in which players kicked a ball toward a goal was probably invented in Ancient China. Many other civilizations had their own ball games, including **Indigenous** peoples of the Americas. A game called football was played in the British Isles for many centuries between different villages. It had few rules and was very dangerous.

RULES OF THE GAME

Football was played in British private schools during the 1800s. Each school had different rules, sometimes allowing players to pick up the ball. In 1863, 12 clubs agreed on a set of rules. This group formed the Football Association (FA) and the game was "association football," or soccer. The game is simply called football in many countries.

The first rules of soccer were very different from the rules used today. The playing field was larger and goals had no crossbars. Players were even allowed to use their hands, although this rule was changed soon after.

In Ancient China, people played a game called cuju. It is considered an early form of soccer.

EARLY LEAGUES

England and Scotland played the first **international** match in 1872. More teams in England's cities started to follow FA rules. Some clubs started to pay the best players and professional soccer was born. In 1888, the first soccer **league** was set up in England. The Scottish Football League followed in 1890.

MEN ONLY

In the early 1900s, large crowds came to watch men's and women's matches. In 1921, the men in charge of English soccer decided that the game was "quite unsuitable" for women. They banned women's matches from being played on major grounds. This made it difficult for women and girls to play in organized teams. The ban lasted until 1971.

The first soccer players wore shirts in team colors, long pants, leather boots, and caps. The first boots or cleats with studs were invented in 1886.

Scottish team, Renton, in 1888

GOING GLOBAL

Soccer soon spread to other countries. The game was played by British workers abroad, or by people who had learned the game in British schools.

Europe's first soccer club outside of England and Scotland was founded in Copenhagen, Denmark, in 1876. The game quickly became popular in many more European countries. In 1904, seven European countries founded the International Federation of Association Football (FIFA). This organization manages soccer around the world.

SOUTH AMERICAN SOCCER

Soccer was played by British workers in Argentina beginning in the 1860s. Charles Miller was born in São Paulo, Brazil, in 1874. He went to study in England, where he learned soccer. When Miller returned to Brazil, his luggage included two soccer balls and a book of rules. In 1895, Miller organized one of the first soccer matches in Brazil. He later set up a league in São Paulo. Miller is known as the father of Brazilian soccer.

Players from Brazil and Sweden during a match held in Rio de Janeiro, Brazil

U.S. SOCCER

In the early 1920s, millions of **immigrants** from Europe brought soccer to the United States. Soccer's early success did not last long. The game failed to match the popularity of baseball and American football, the national sports in the United States.

FIRST WORLD CUP

Soccer was first played at the Olympic Games in 1900. Professional players were not allowed in the Olympics. Soccer needed its own global competition. The first World Cup was held in Uruguay in 1930. Thirteen teams took part. Many European countries stayed away, concerned about the cost and time needed to travel by ship to South America. Uruguay beat Argentina in the final. The United States reached the semifinals of the men's World Cup for the only time.

Crowds packed the stadium in Uruguay to watch the 1930 World Cup.

AT THE MATCH

Large crowds were part of soccer from the 1880s onward. Supporters were mostly men, standing to watch with no protection from the weather. This was very different compared to the modern stadiums that today's fans enjoy.

CHAMPIONS AND CHALLENGES

Global soccer started to take shape as we know it today in the 1950s. The World Cup became the tournament every national team dreamed of winning.

WORLD CUP DREAMS

Brazil **hosted** the tournament in 1950, expecting to win. They lost to Uruguay in front of possibly the biggest soccer crowd of all time. The bruised Brazilians recovered to win three World Cups in 1958, 1962, and 1970, with a brilliant team led by the dazzling skills of Pelé.

As well as Brazil, other European and South American teams dominated the World Cup. It was the biggest stage for stars such as England's Geoff Hurst, who scored three goals in the final of 1966. Argentina's Diego Maradona inspired his team to victory in 1986. West Germany was often the team to beat, reaching the final six times and winning three World Cups between 1954 and 1990.

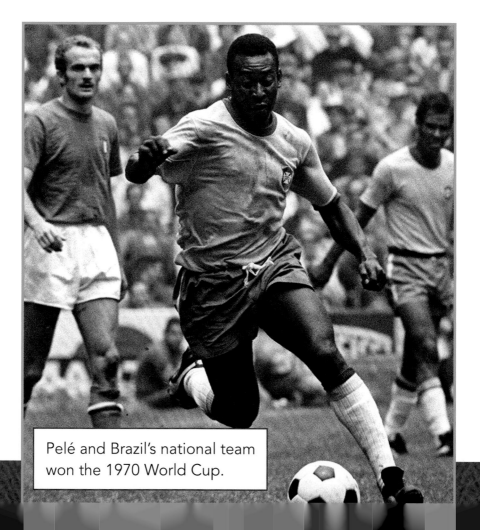

Pelé and Brazil's national team won the 1970 World Cup.

A GLOBAL AUDIENCE

In 1954, World Cup matches from Switzerland were shown live on TV across many countries for the first time. But most people did not yet own a TV to watch them. Later, the growth of TV would bring this festival of soccer into homes around the world.

EUROPEAN CUP

The World Cup is not the only competition between players from different countries. The first European Cup was won by Real Madrid in 1956. This competition brought together Europe's biggest clubs, from Manchester United to AC Milan, and many of the greatest players.

Real Madrid dominated the first years of the European Cup. In the 1970s, Dutch and German clubs led the way. Between 1977 and 1984, English clubs Nottingham Forest won twice, and Liverpool won the Cup four times. Traveling by airplane made it possible for teams to travel across Europe and millions of viewers watched the matches on TV.

Liverpool celebrates winning the European Cup.

FAN VIOLENCE AND DISASTERS

Fan violence and stadium safety became major problems for soccer in the 1970s and 1980s. In 1985, a wall collapsed due to rioting at the European Cup final between Liverpool and Juventus. As a result, 39 Juventus fans died. In 1989, 97 Liverpool fans were killed in a stadium crush. Crumbling stadiums and fighting fans turned many people against soccer. Could the game recover?

GLOBAL FANS

At the start of the 1990s, soccer had to change. The game needed to attract new supporters after the problems of the 1980s. New players wanted to join the global game too.

The growth of satellite and cable TV channels meant there was more soccer on TV than ever before. Fans could now watch Real Madrid or Manchester United from anywhere in the world. This attracted new fans to the game.

Heysel Stadium in Brussels, Belgium, before the 1985 European Cup final

USA 1994

In 1994, the World Cup took place in the United States for the first time. Many people wondered if the event would be successful. The United States did not even have a professional soccer league at that time. Huge crowds came to watch the World Cup. It led to the founding of Major League Soccer.

The Rose Bowl in Pasadena, California, hosted the 1994 World Cup final.

WOMEN'S SOCCER REBORN

For many years, people in charge of soccer had ignored half the population—women and girls. That started to change in the 1970s when rules that restricted women's teams were changed. The first women's international match, between France and the Netherlands, was played in 1971.

International tournaments in the 1980s attracted new teams and fans to women's soccer. The first Women's World Cup was organized in 1991. The United States beat China in the final. The U.S. Women's National Team starred Mia Hamm and Michelle Akers. This team also won the first Olympic soccer competition in 1996.

Mia Hamm (left) during the 1991 World Cup

NEW STARS ON THE SCENE

Before 1990, most of soccer's biggest stars came from Europe or South America. But the major clubs now started to look further for talented players. New stars, including George Weah and Abedi Pele, came from Africa to play in Europe. Young players saw local heroes playing in Europe and believed that they could do the same. By 2000, there were nearly 1,000 Africans playing in European leagues.

As the best young players moved to the biggest teams, this was not always good for fans in other countries. Their favorite player could be playing on another continent. The most talented players could only be seen on TV and never played for local teams.

Two of the greatest players of the 1990s and 2000s were Brazil's brilliant goal scorer Ronaldo and French master Zinedine Zidane. Each was crowned World Player of the Year three times between 1996 and 2003.

Abedi Pele during
a match in 1996

NEW HORIZONS

Professional soccer started as a game based around cities and clubs. Working people would watch their local team on a Saturday. Today, a supporter of Arsenal or Barcelona could be in China or Egypt, able to watch every game on a TV or cell phone.

GLOBAL GOALS

Soccer has continued to find new fans around the world. The World Cup hosts in 2002 were Japan and South Korea. This was the first time that soccer's biggest tournament had been staged in Asia. Local fans were most excited by the South Korean team reaching the semifinals. In 2010, South Africa brought the World Cup to Africa for the first time, a continent with millions of fans and some of the world's best players.

The 2026 men's World Cup will be held in three different countries. It returns to the United States and Mexico, and Canada will host the tournament for the first time.

Carlos Salcido of Mexico and Teko Modise of South Africa during a 2010 World Cup match in Johannesburg, South Africa

Women's soccer has reached new heights since the first global competitions of the 1990s. The Women's World Cup grows more popular every four years, with Spain winning the 2023 tournament in Australia and New Zealand. The first professional women's league started in the United States in 2001. Many other countries now have their own leagues as well.

Spain celebrates their 2023 World Cup win.

CHANGING TECHNOLOGY

Soccer is a simple game, but technology has brought many changes to professional soccer. Coaches track their players using **GPS** technology. It can show how far and how fast they move throughout a game. Technology also supports refereeing decisions. Cameras and tracking technology show whether a player is **offside** or if the ball has crossed the goal line.

A GPS tracker is attached to German player Fabienne Dongus.

The number of boys and girls playing soccer in U.S. high schools has increased four times in the past 40 years and now stands at 800,000.

SOCCER'S FUTURE

The people who first set the rules of soccer in 1863 could not have imagined what the game would become. Soccer has touched every corner of the world. Soccer clubs began as part of local neighborhoods. The biggest clubs are now owned by billionaires from around the world. New teams and brilliant players will continue to amaze those who love the game.

PART OF THE TEAM

Soccer clubs and star players continue to attract more fans and win trophies. But the story of soccer remains quite simple for many people. The game lets millions of people develop their skills and physical fitness. Players find friendship and fun playing as a team on the pitch.

Superstar Lionel Messi in action for Inter Miami

Soccer players celebrate a win in Cape Town, South Africa.

GLOSSARY

GPS (GEE-pee-ess)—stands for Global Positioning System; an electronic tool used to find the location of an object

host (HOST)—a person or organization receiving others as guests; the country where a World Cup is played is the host

immigrant (IM-uh-gruhnt)—a person who moves to a different country to live

Indigenous (IN-di-juh-nss)—people who first lived in a place

international (in-tur-NASH-uh-nuhl)—including more than one country

league (LEEG)—a group of teams that play against each other regularly

offside (OFF-syd)—a soccer rule; a player is offside if they are ahead of the last defender in the opponent's half when the ball is played to them by a teammate

professional (pruh-FESH-uh-nuhl)—a person who makes money by doing an activity that other people might do without pay

READ MORE

Allen, Jules. *Mexico vs. the United States.* North Mankato, MN: Capstone, 2023.

DK. *Eyewitness Soccer.* New York: Penguin, 2023.

Scheff, Matt. *The World Cup: Soccer's Greatest Tournament.* Minneapolis: Lerner Publishing Group, 2021.

INTERNET SITES

FIFA: 1930 FIFA World Cup Uruguay
fifa.com/tournaments/mens/worldcup/1930uruguay

Sports Illustrated Kids: Soccer
sikids.com/tag/soccer

U.S. Soccer: U.S. Soccer Timeline
ussoccer.com/history/timeline

INDEX

ABOUT THE AUTHOR

Nick Hunter has written more than 100 books for young people. He specializes in writing about history, social studies, and sports. Nick lives in Oxford, UK, with his wife and two sports-loving sons. His favorite soccer teams are Norwich City and England.